Same Love

Coloring Book

Adult Colouring Books

Aryla Publishing 2018

978-1-912675-18-0

www.arylapublishing.com

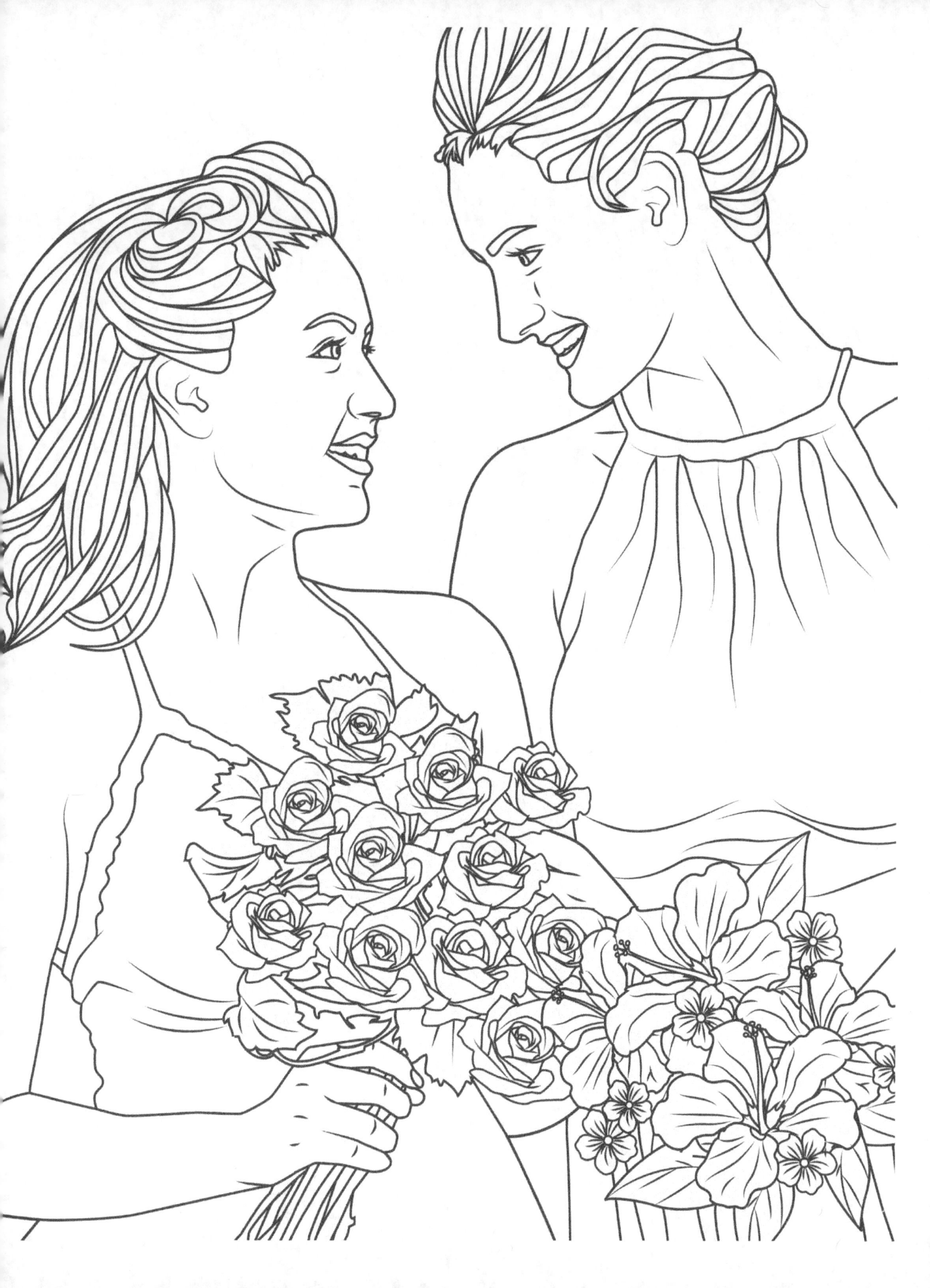

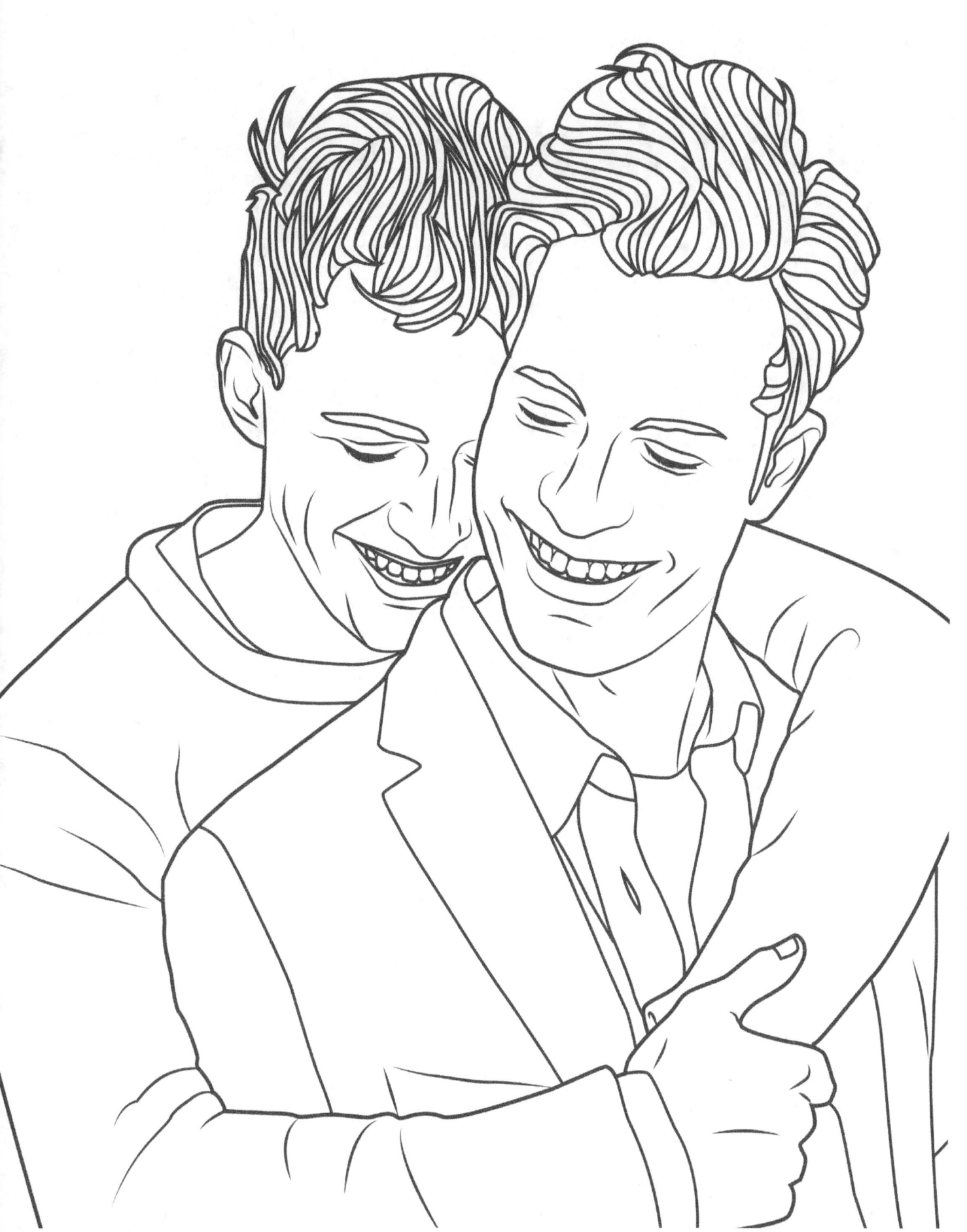

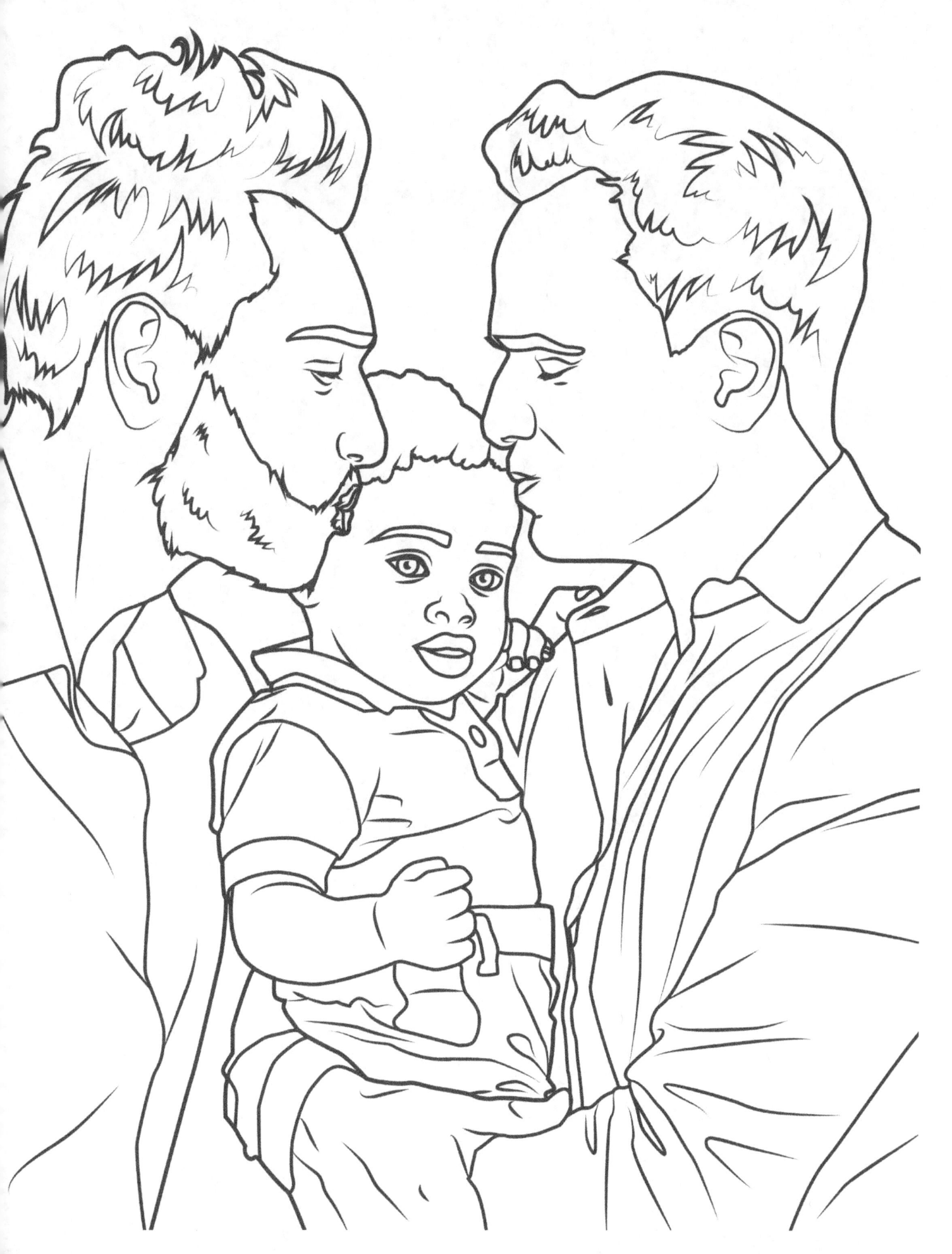

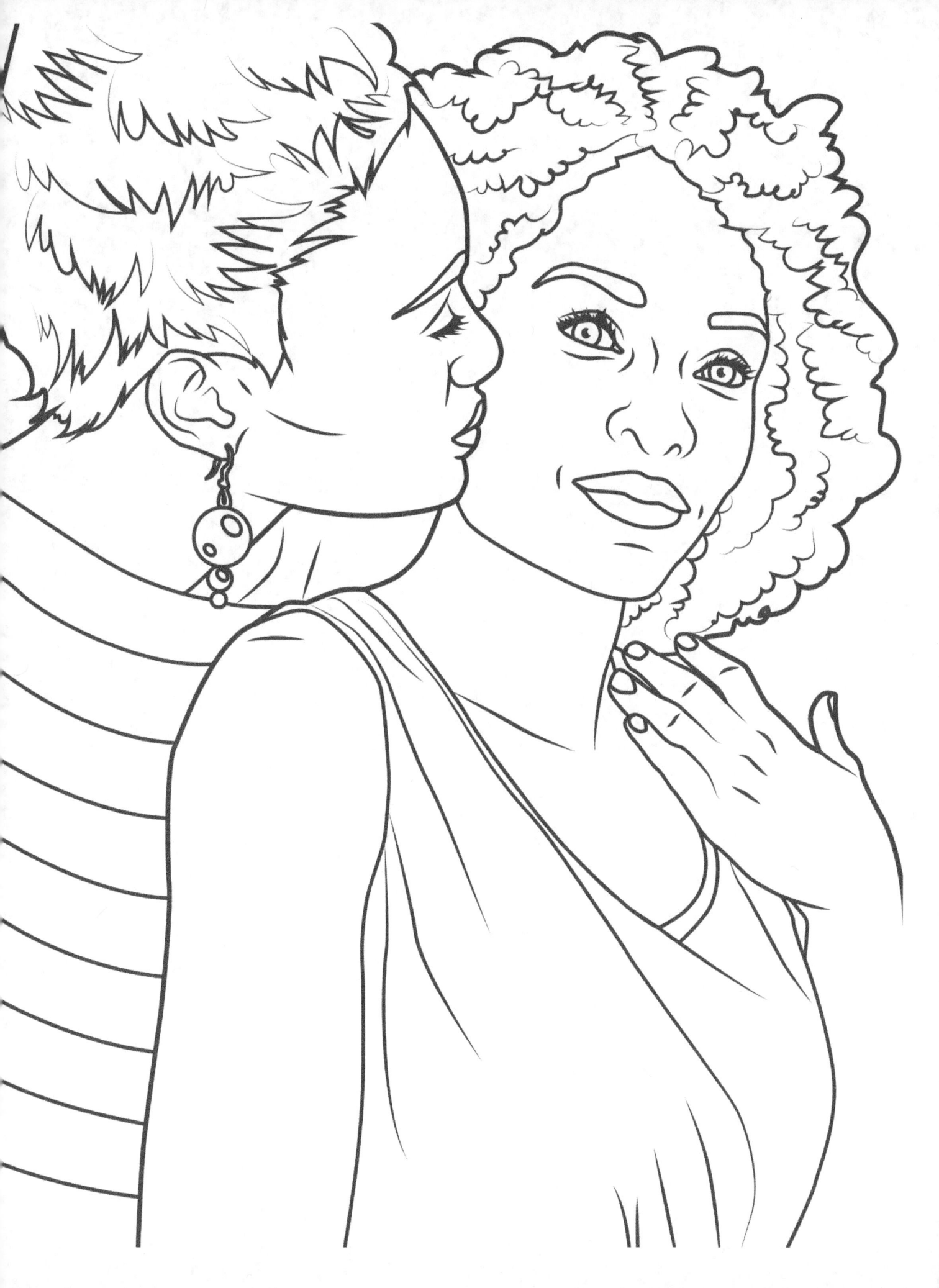

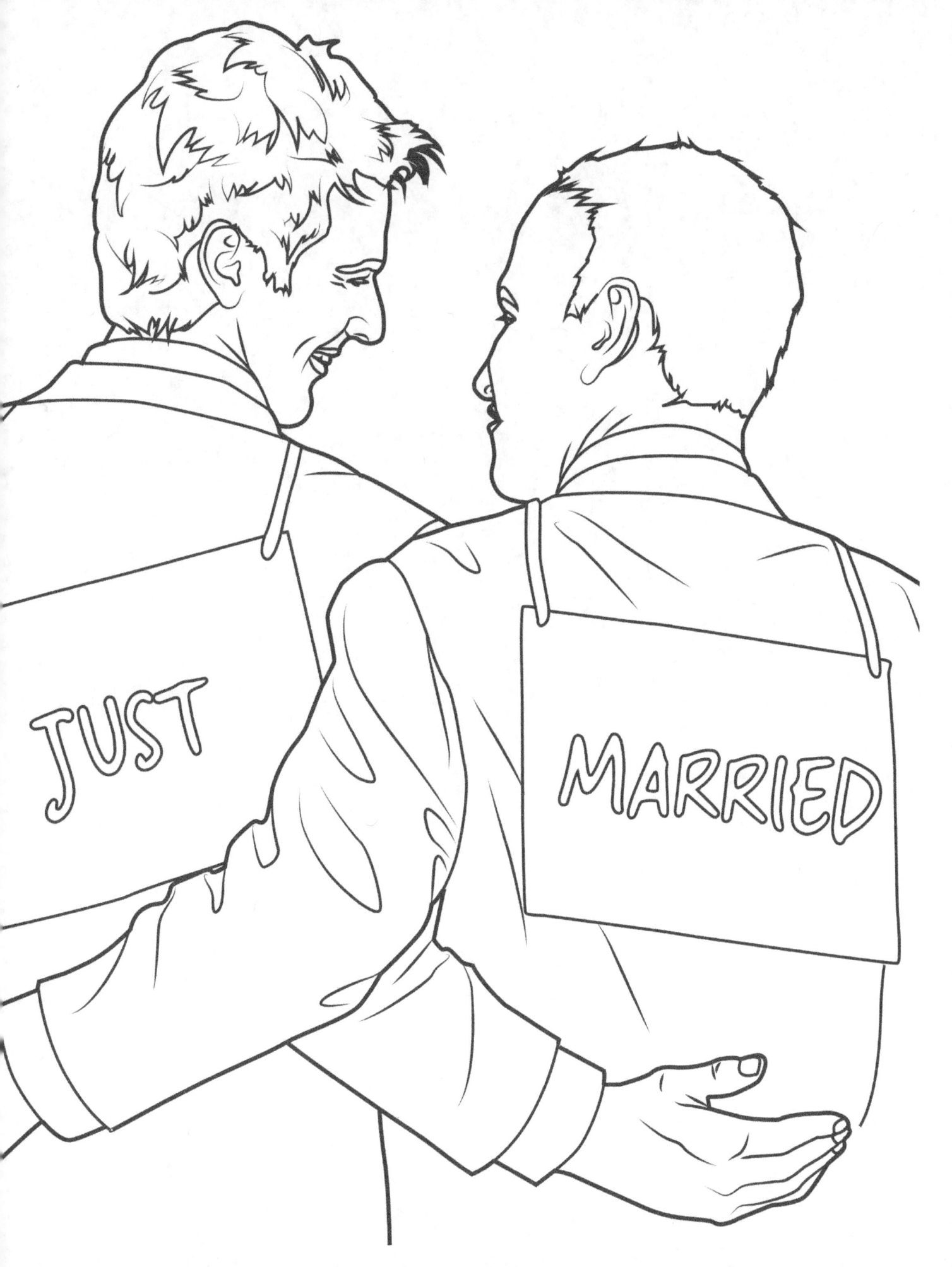

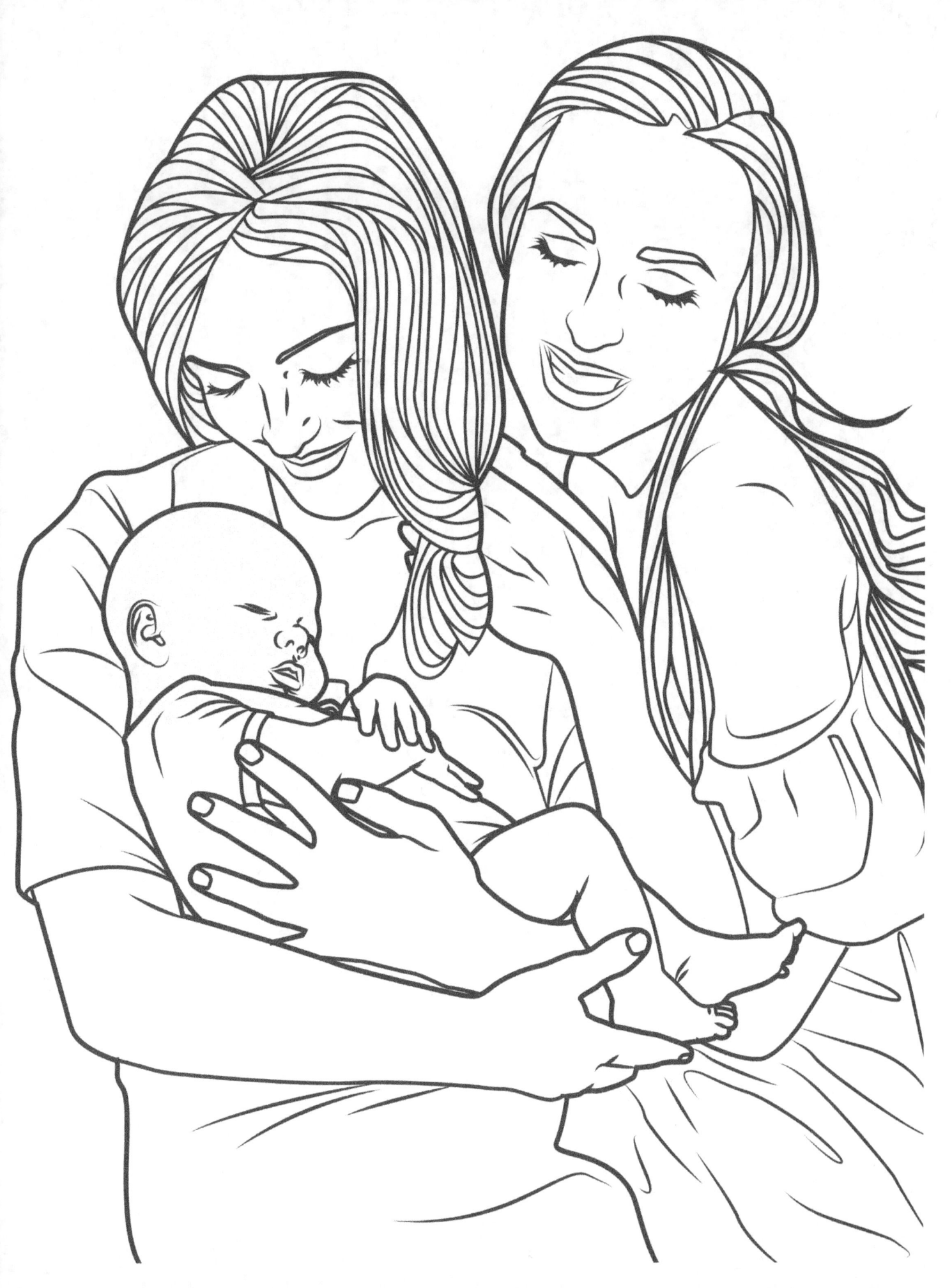

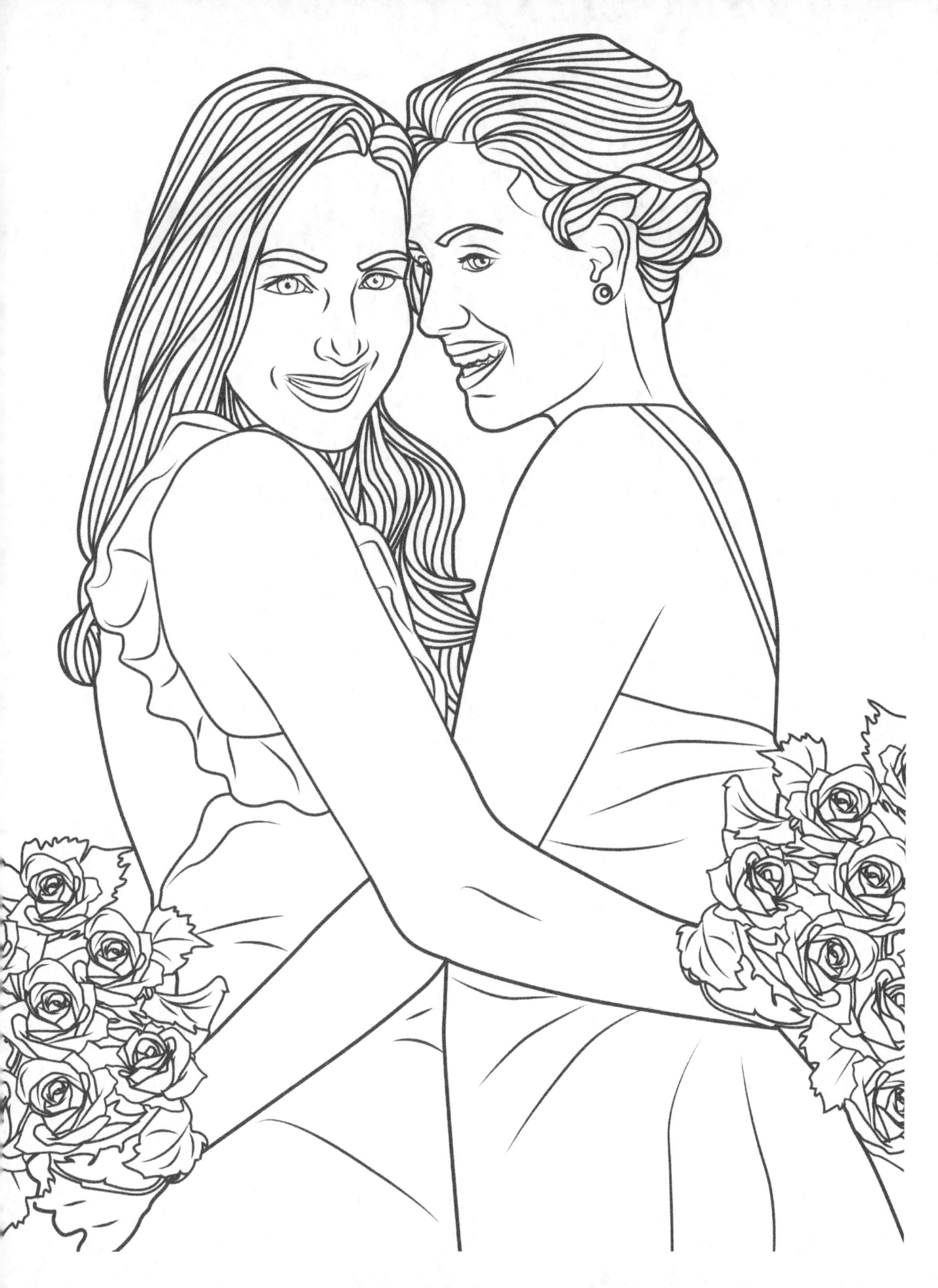

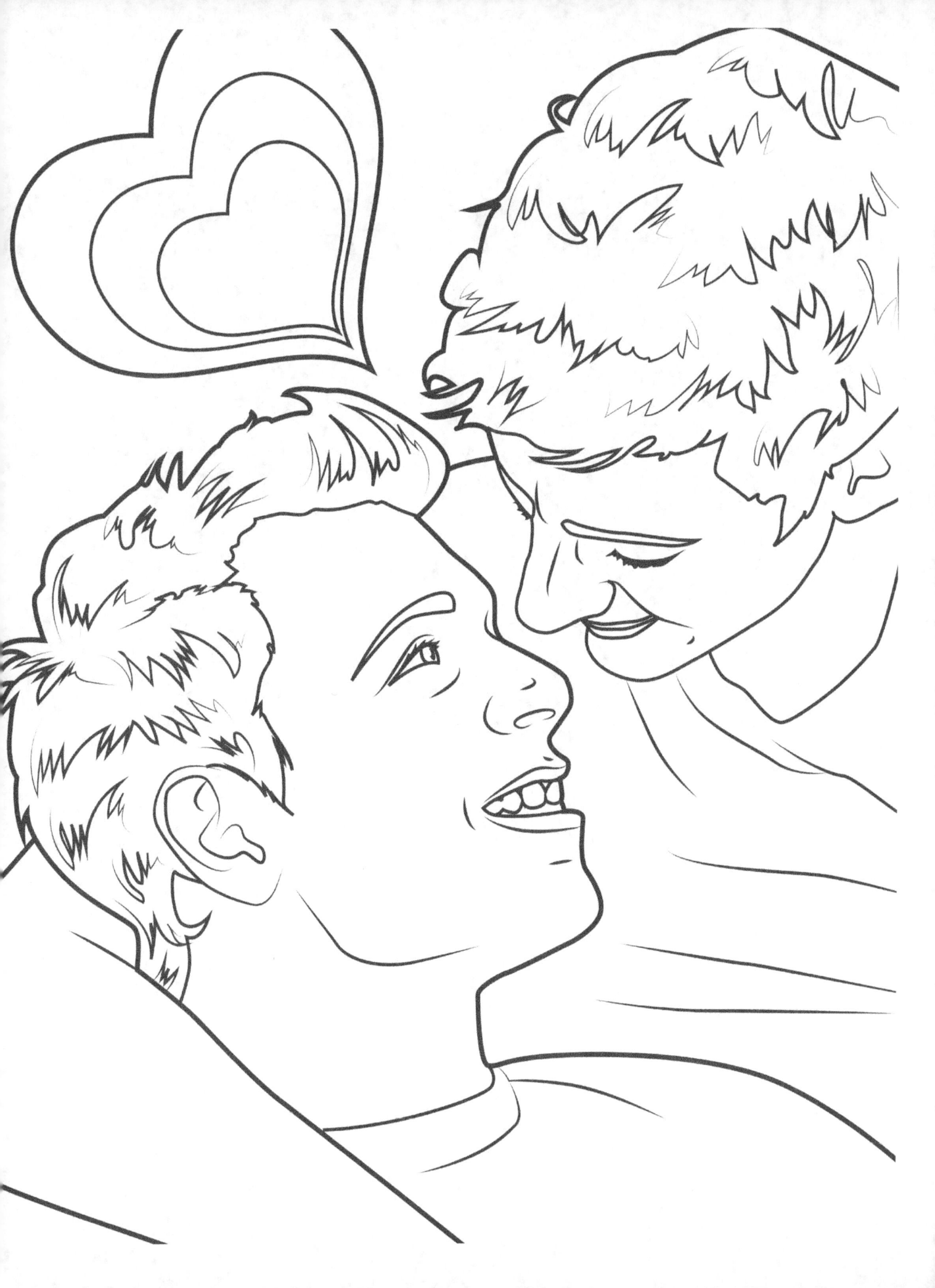

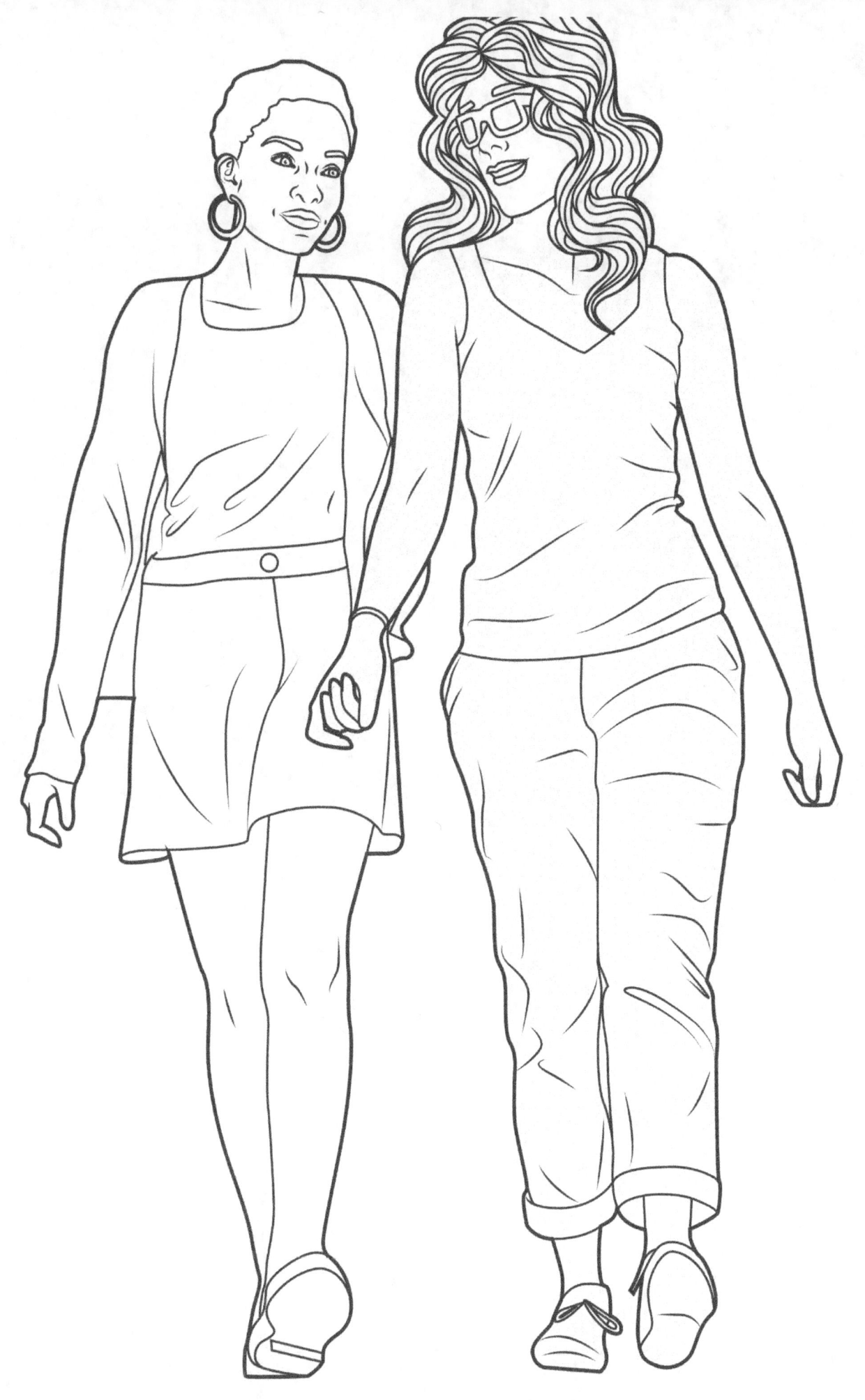

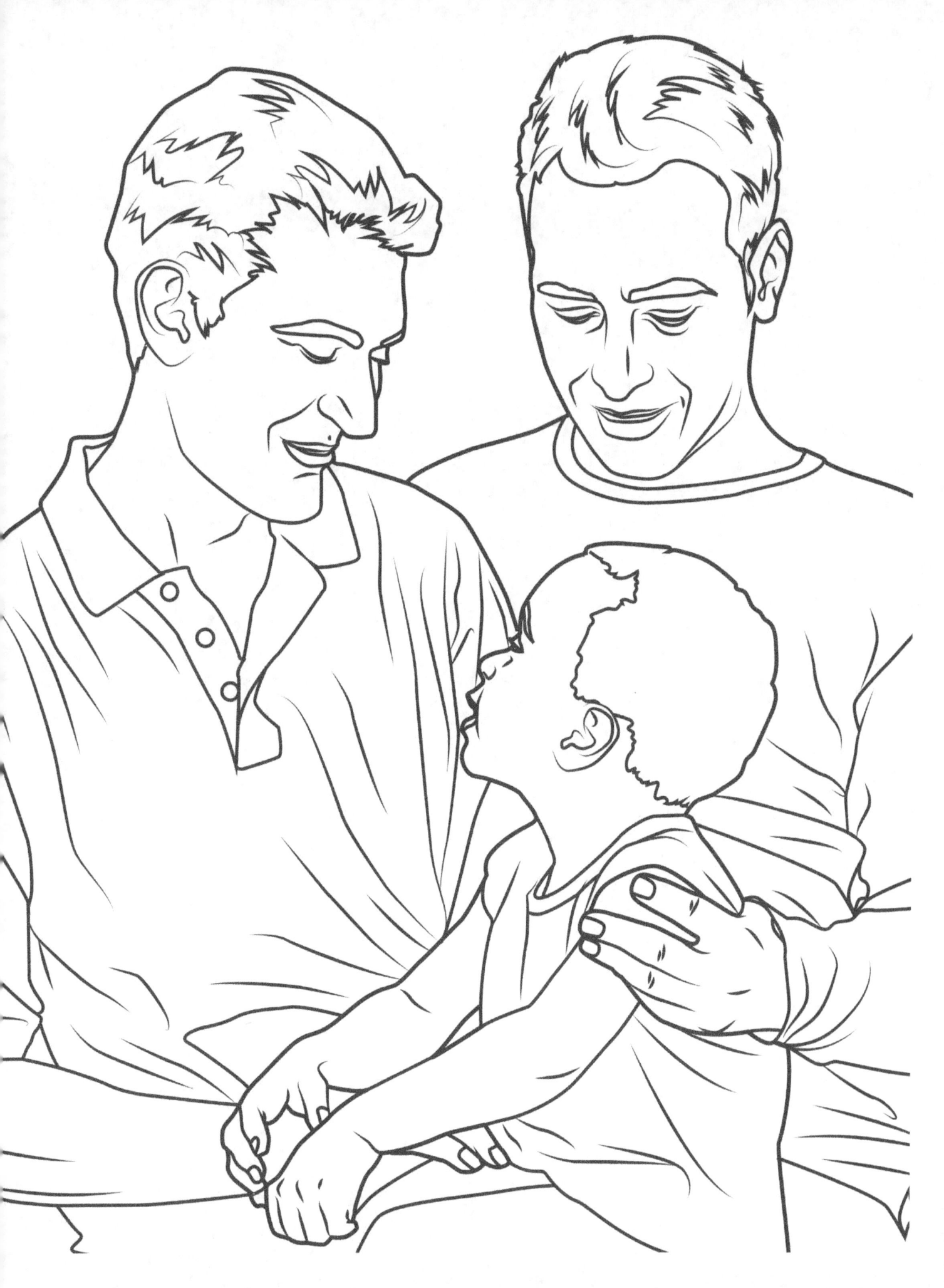

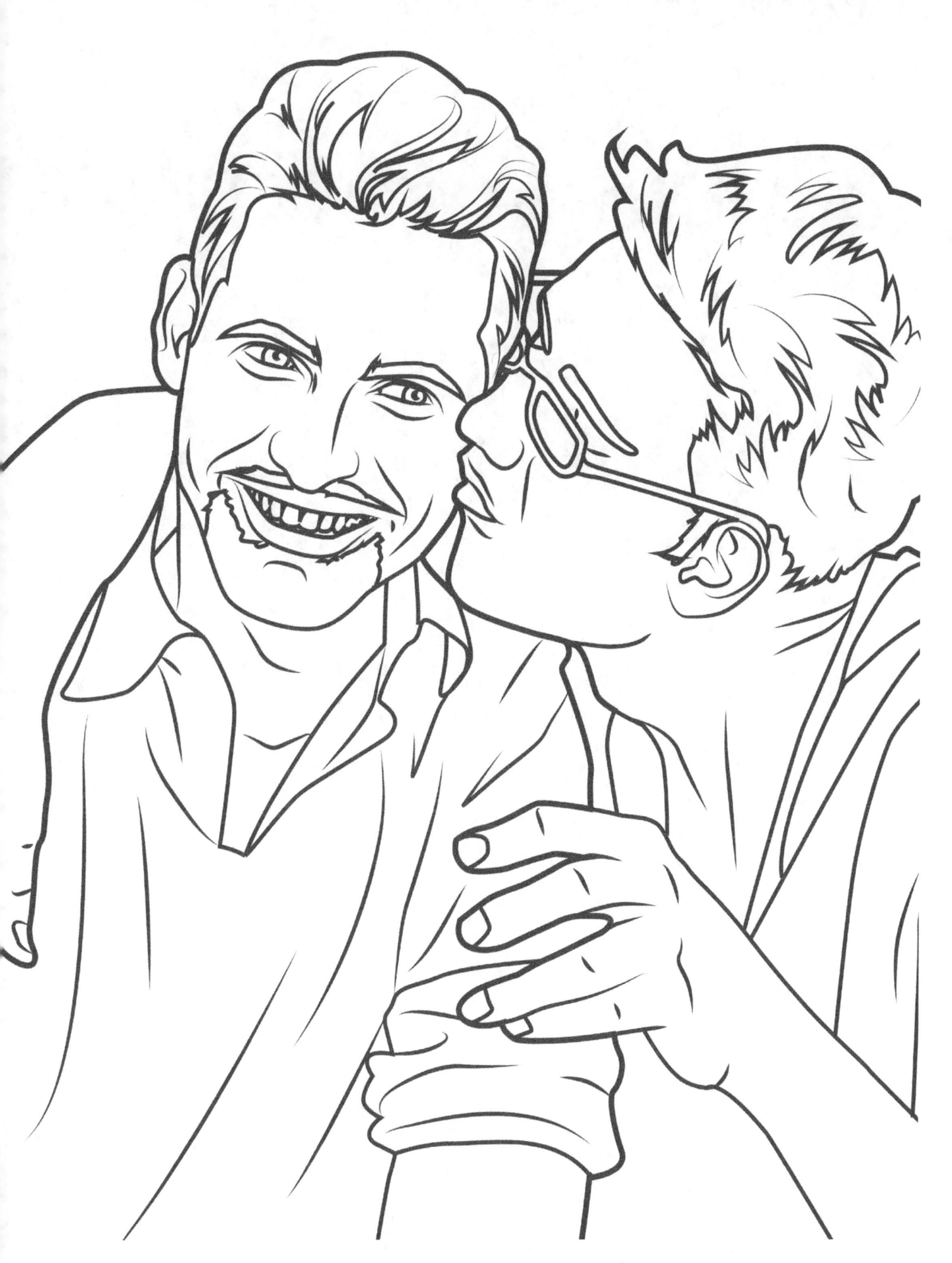

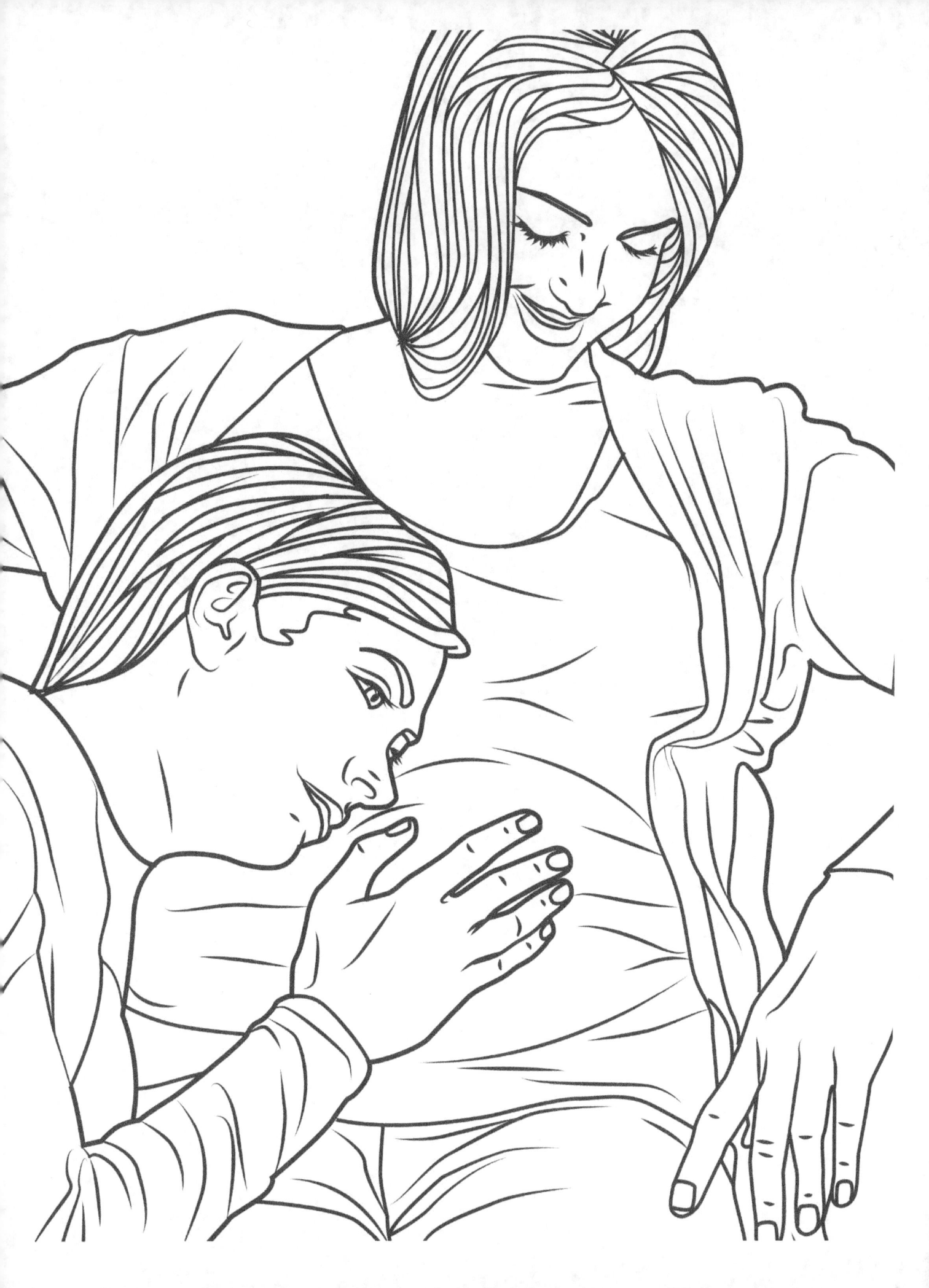

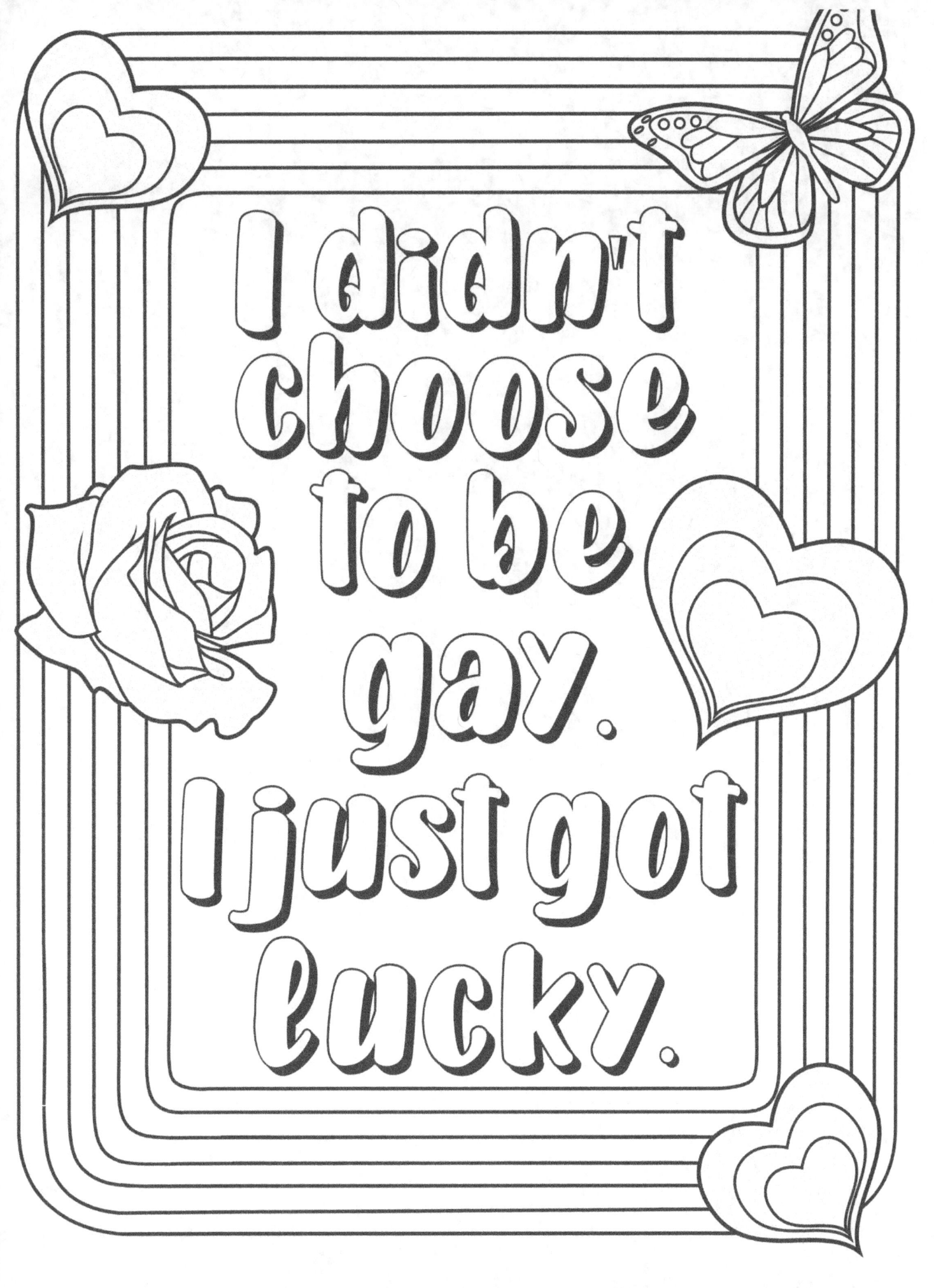

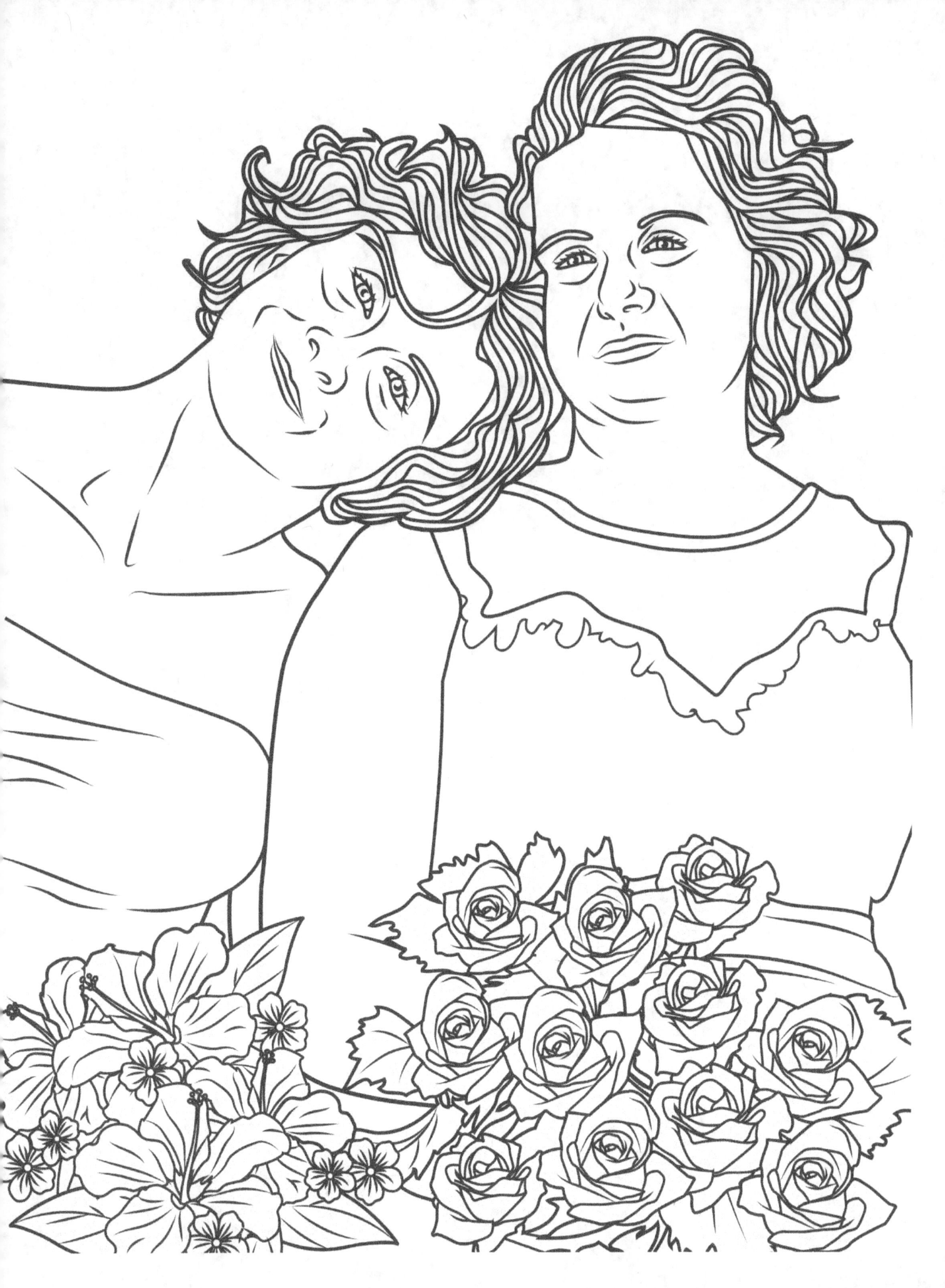

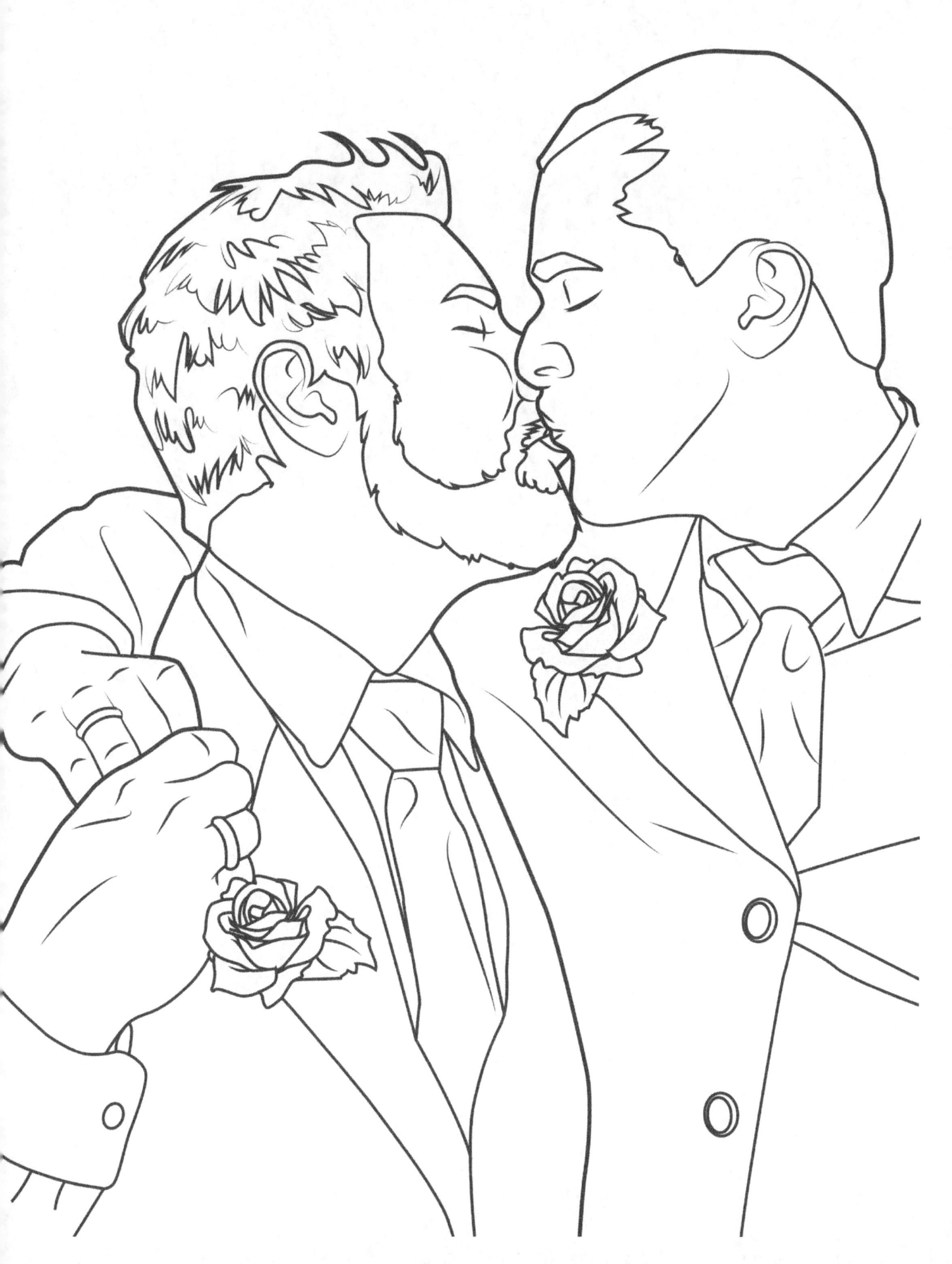

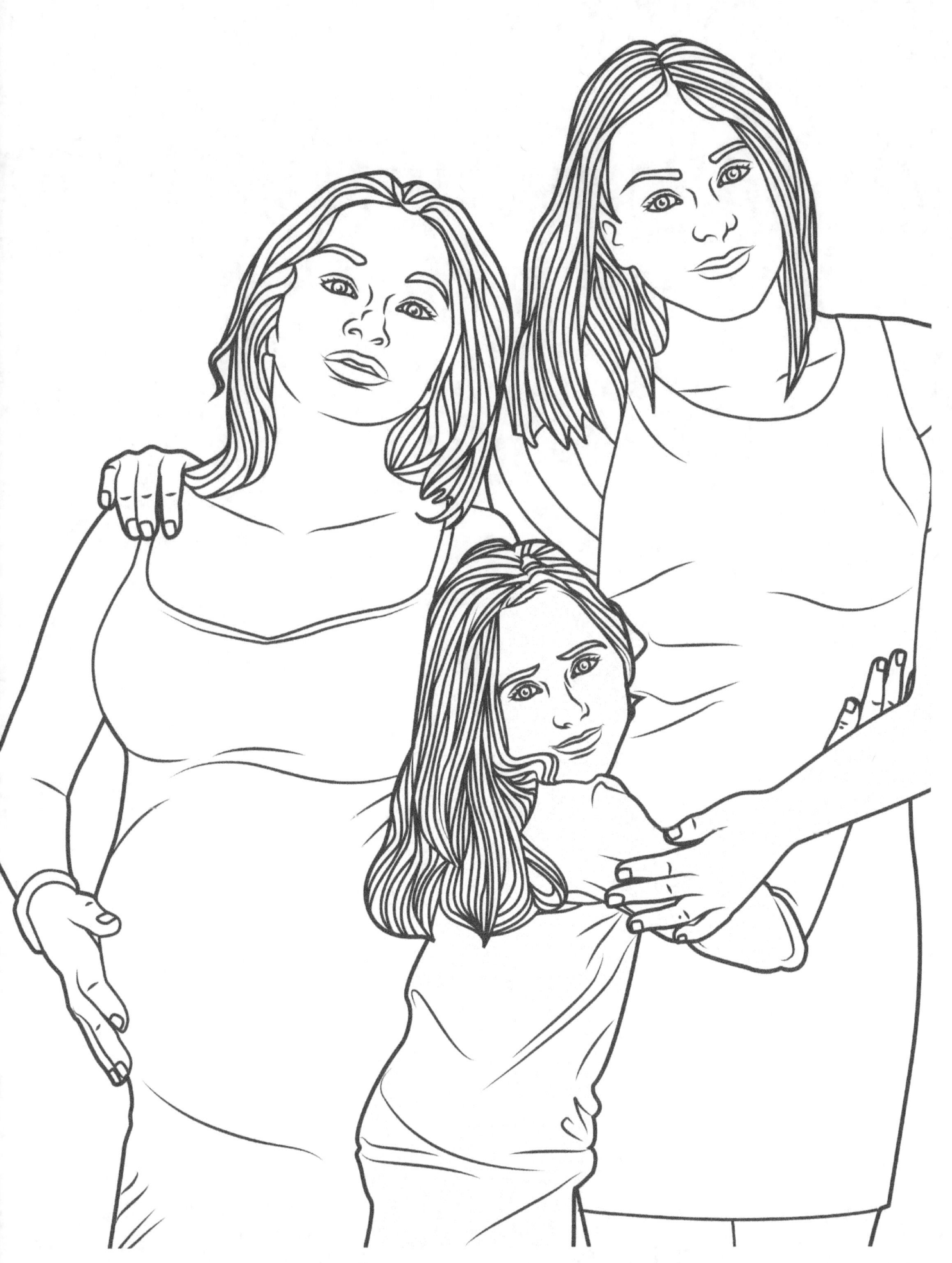

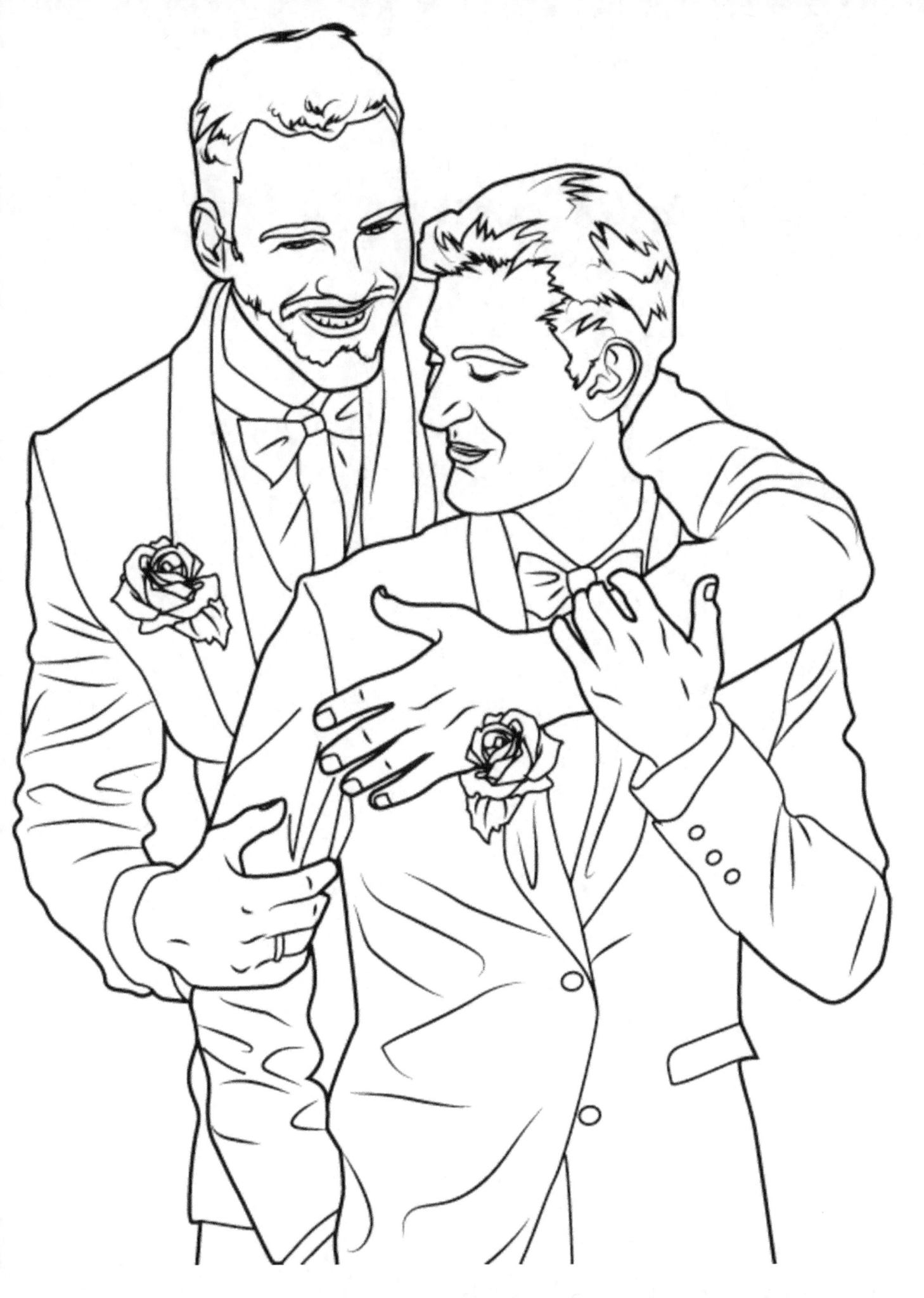

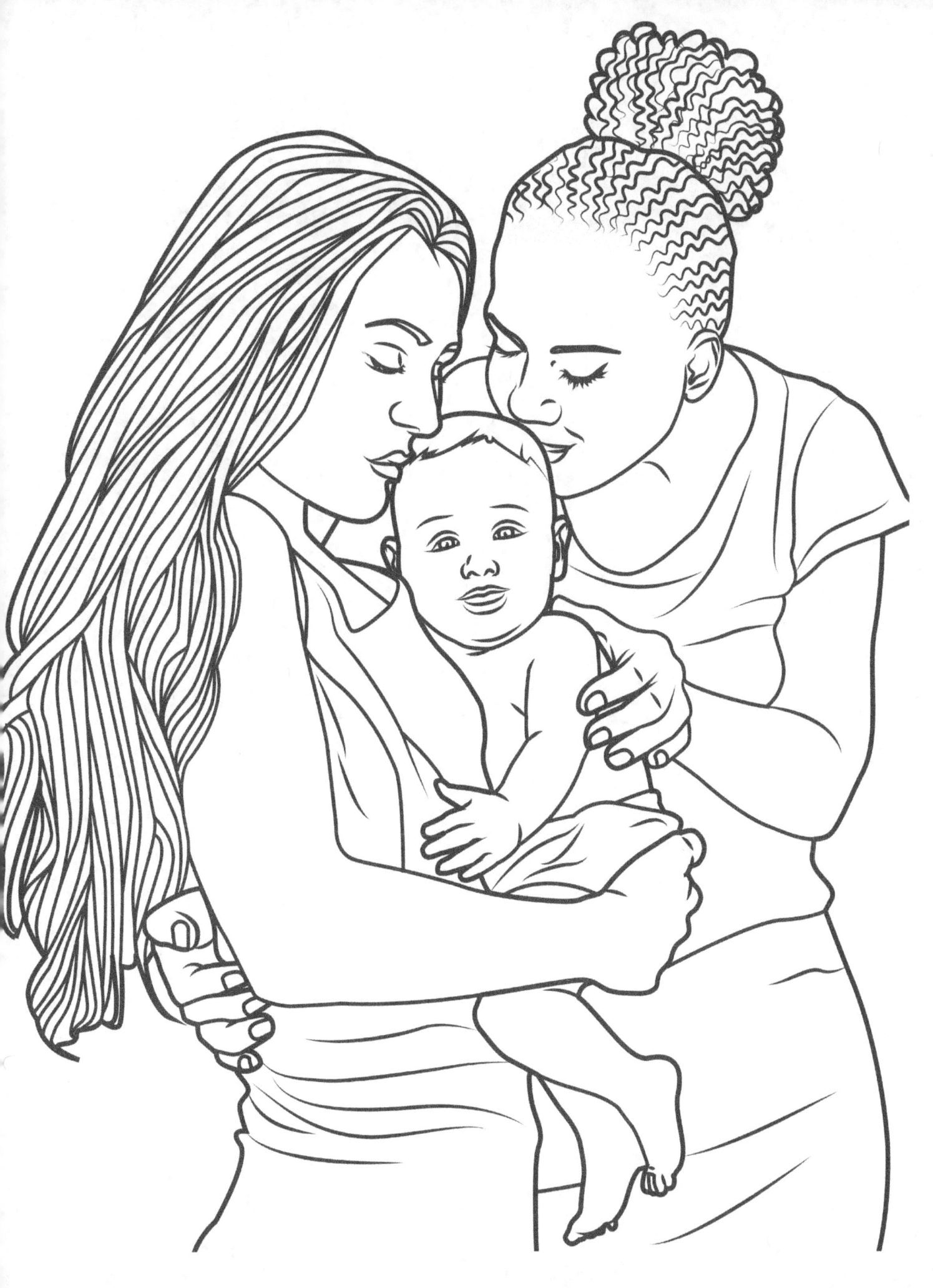

LOVE IS TOO BEAUTIFUL TO BE HIDDEN IN THE CLOSET

As long as you are Happy does it matter who you fall in Love with?

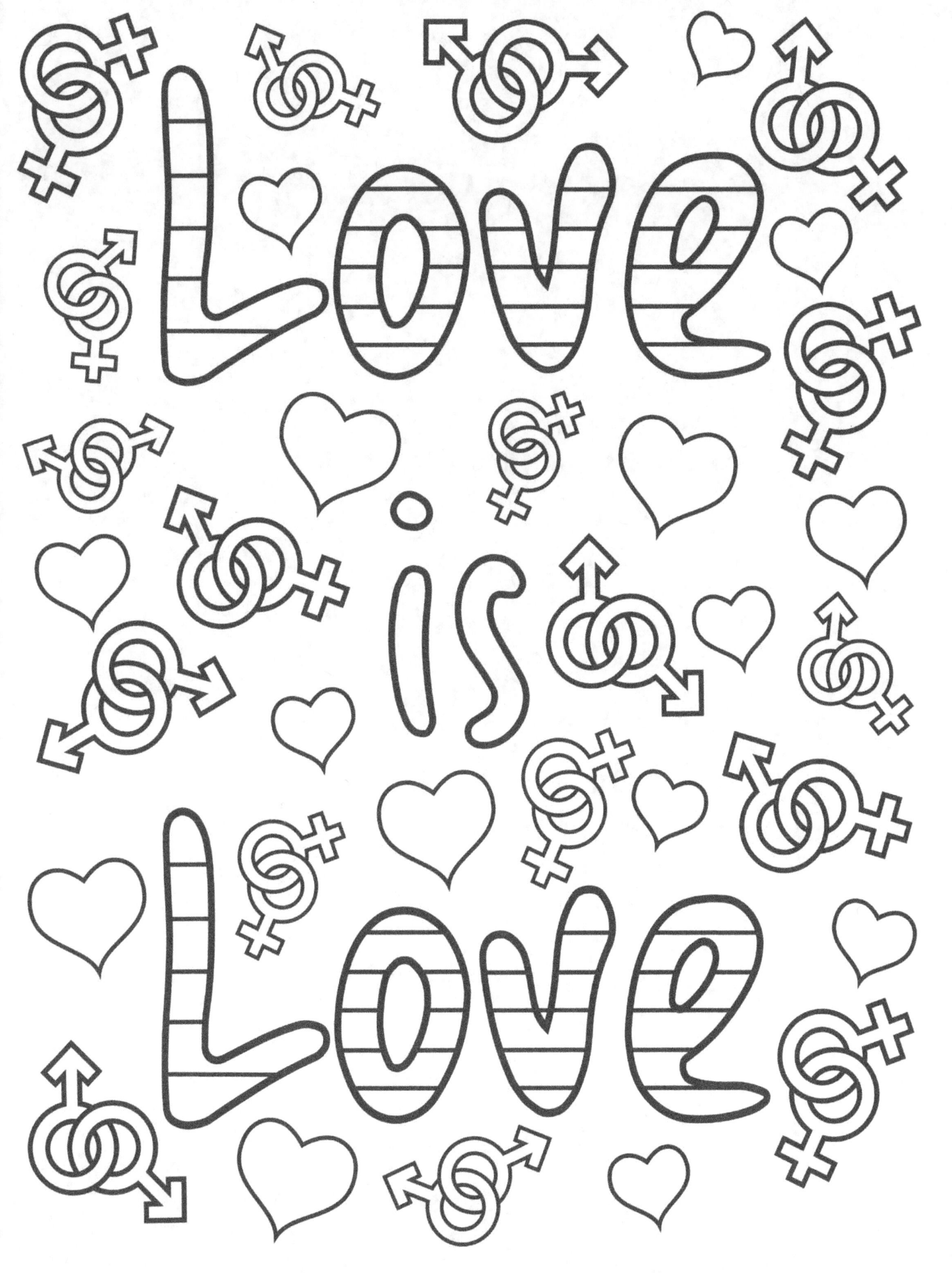

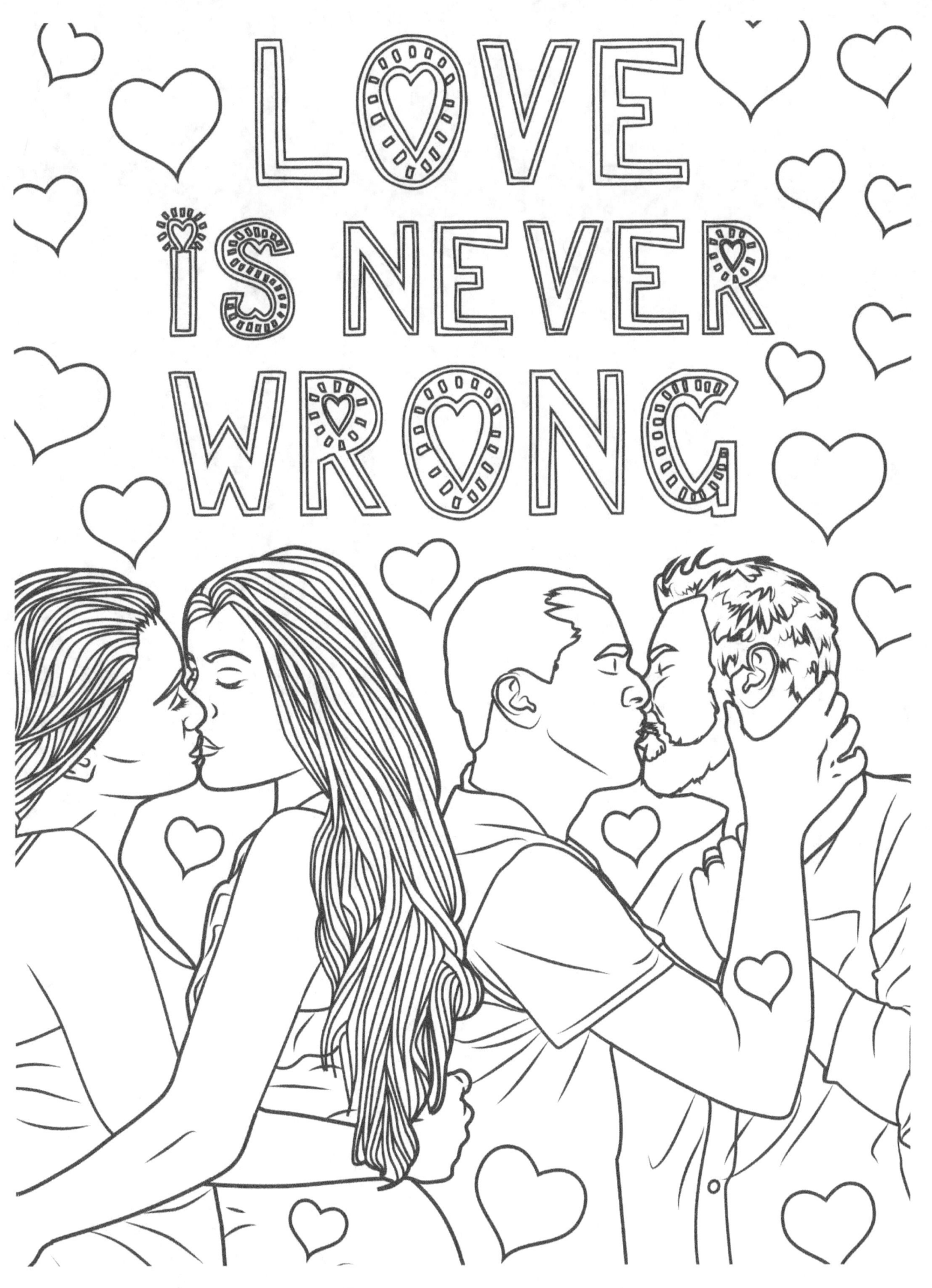

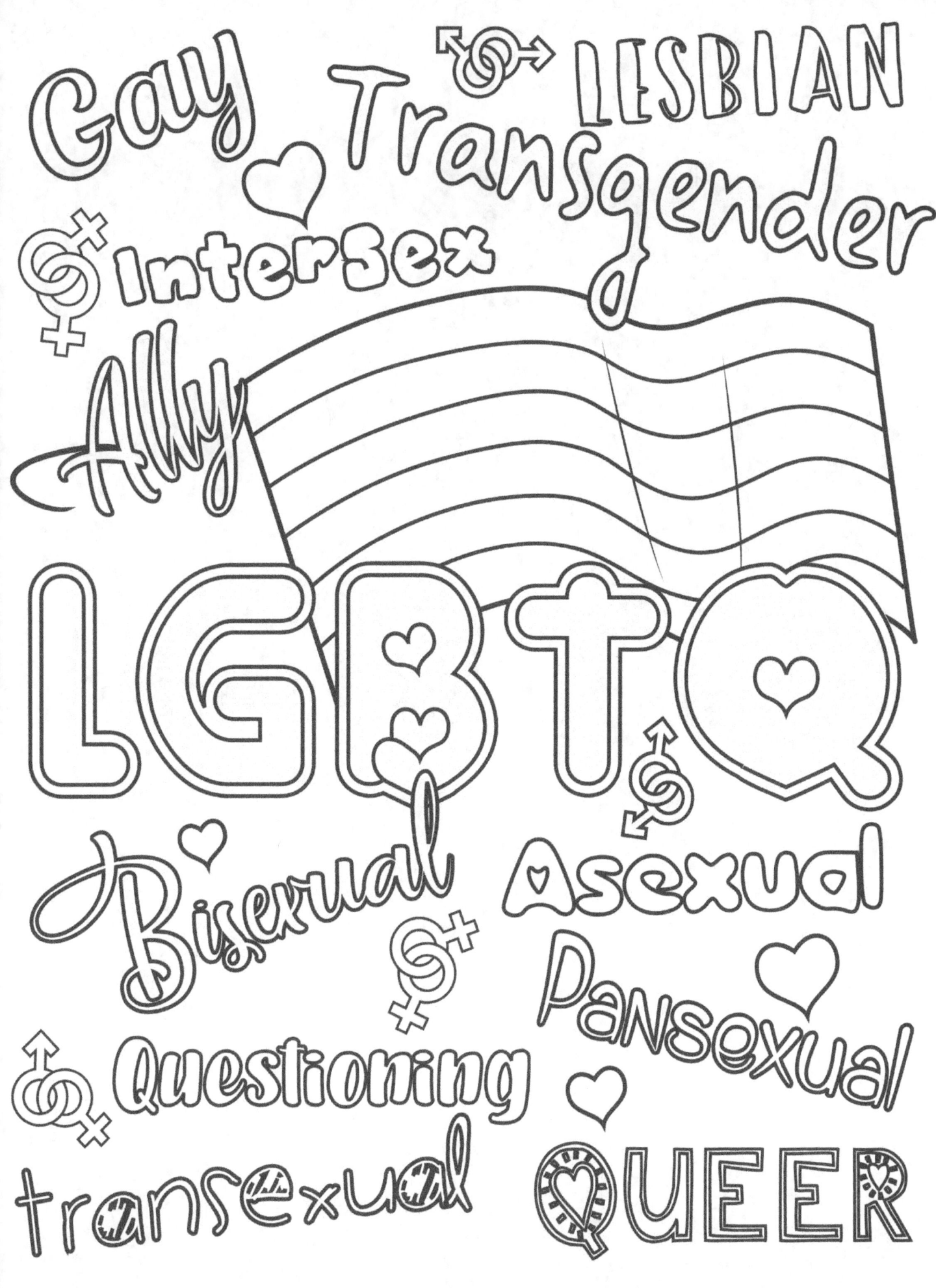

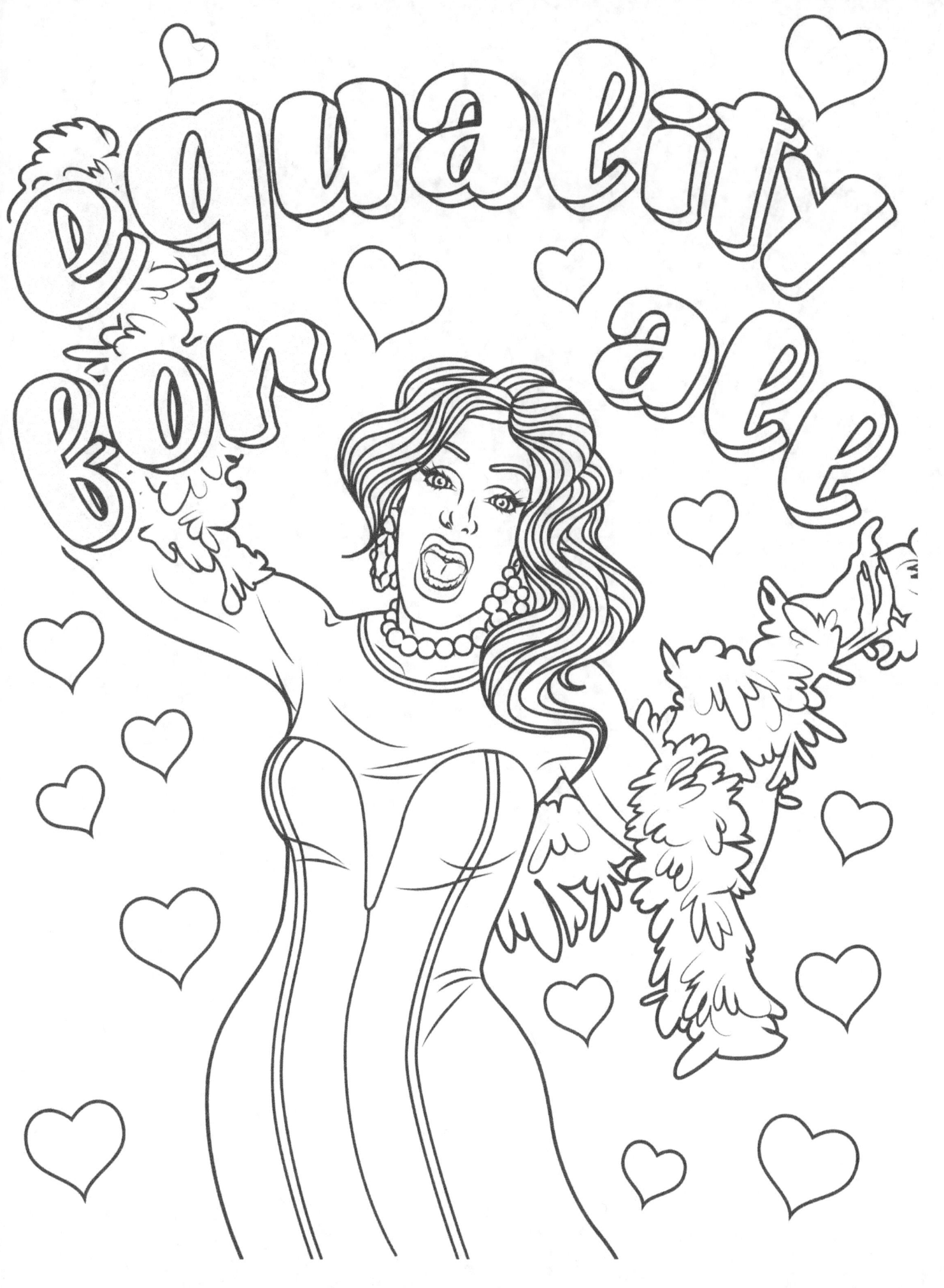

Thank you for purchasing this book.

If you would like to know more about Aryla Publishing Books please visit:-

www.ArylaPublishing.com

Or follow us on
Facebook
Twitter
Instagram
for *free promotions*

@arylapublishing

We would love to know what you think of this book so please leave us a review.

Have a wonderful day ☺

Other Coloring Books from Aryla Publishing

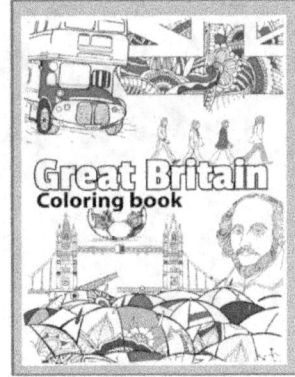
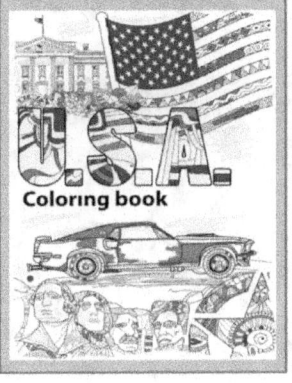
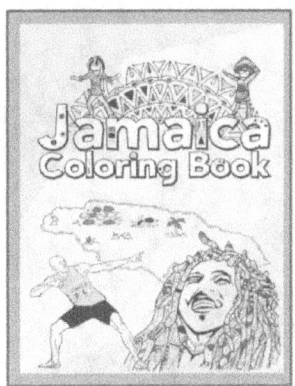
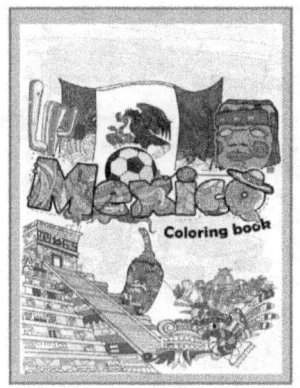

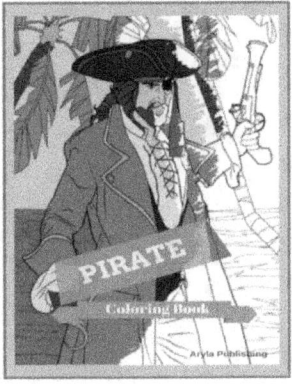
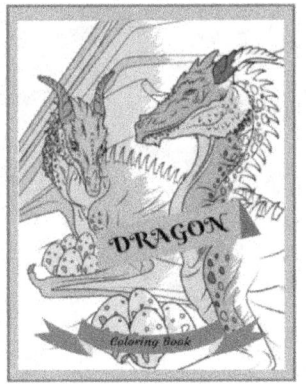
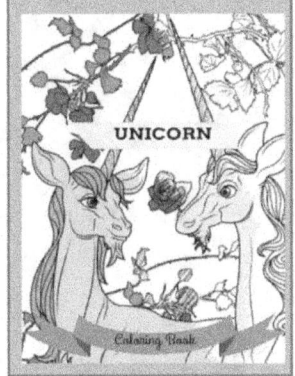
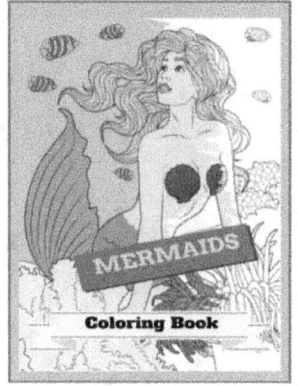

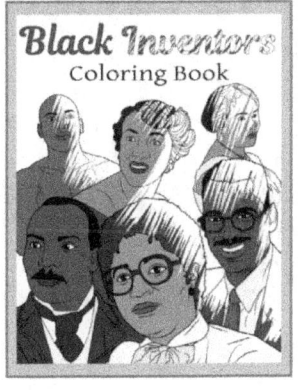
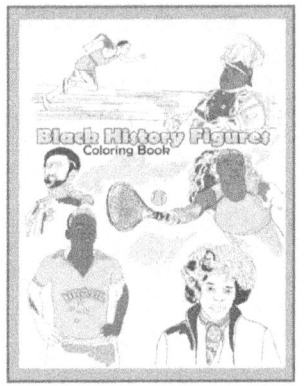
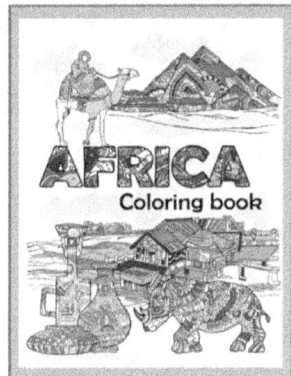
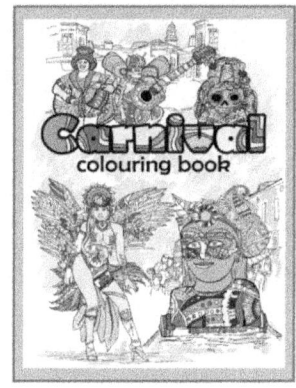

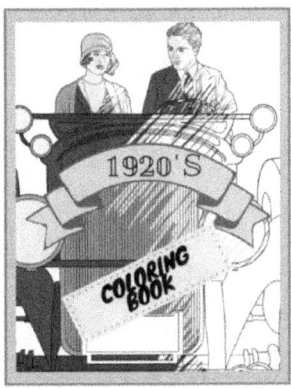
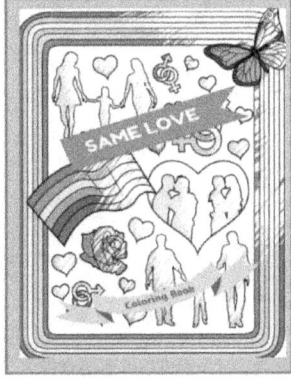
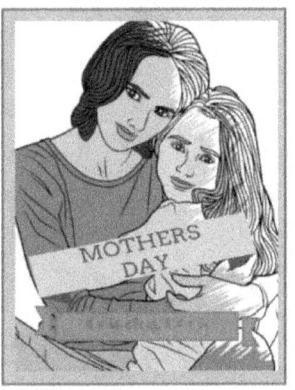
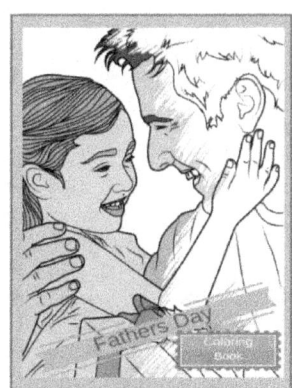

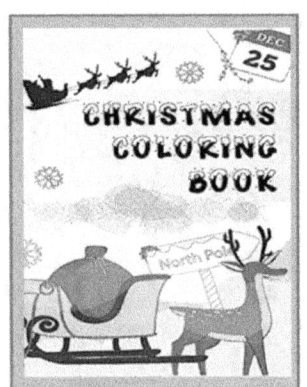
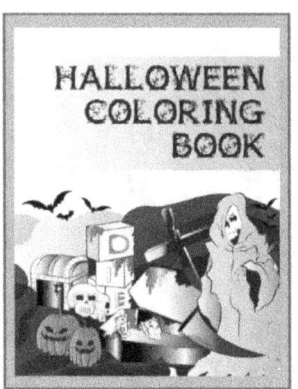
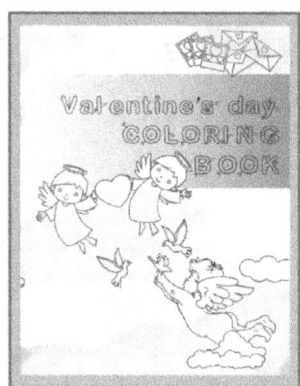
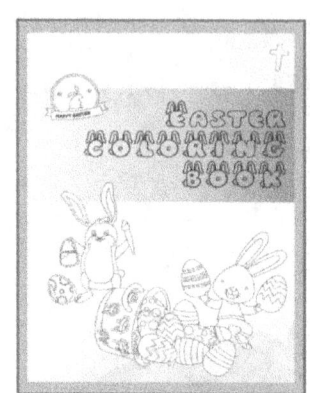